PARALEGAL'S
JOURNAL

Stealth Journals

Jamie Davis Whitmer is a freelance virtual paralegal.

This journal is designed with prompts to help keep you focused and motivated throughout your day. Jamie has found that she is most effective if she first only focuses on three medium-to-large sized work projects per day, and thought that you might be the same! The blank lines in the beginning of the book represent an indexing system to aid in reflection and planning throughout the year.

Jamie has often thought to herself: "I document, therefore I am." It is her hope that this journal not only makes you feel better about your progress at work, but that it will also serve as a useful tool for you for performance evaluations.

In a time when everyone's electronic data is subject to compromise, Stealth Journals is a company that is committed to providing you tools to maintain your privacy.

The software you use at work to manage tasks and deadlines cannot be relied upon to measure your contributions or value. What of your individual accomplishments? If you do not personally note them, it is the same as though they never existed.

We must make records. We must prove what we have done, and what we can do.

www.stealthjournals.com

IF FOUND RETURN TO:

Name:

_____

Firm:

_____

_____

_____

Email:

_____

Cell:

_____

13. _____

14. _____

15. _____

16. _____

17. _____

18. _____

19. _____

20. _____

21. _____

22. _____

23. _____

24. _____

25. _____

26. _____

27. _____

28. _____

29. _____

30. _____

31. _____

32. _____

33. _____

34. _____

35. _____

36. _____

37. _____

38. _____

39. _____

40. _____

41. _____

42. _____

43. _____

44. _____

45. _____

46. _____

47. _____

48. _____

49. _____

50. _____

51. _____

52. _____

53. _____

54. _____

55. _____

56. _____

57. _____

58. _____

59. _____

60. _____

61.

62.

63.

64.

65.

66.

67.

68.

69.

70.

71.

72.

73.

74.

75.

76.

77.

78.

79.

80.

81.

82.

83.

84.

85.

86.

87.

88.

89.

90.

91.

92.

93.

94.

95.

96.

97.

98.

99.

100.

101.

102.

103.

104.

105.

106.

107.

108.

109.

110.

111.

112.

113.

114.

115.

116.

117.

118.

119.

120.

121.

122.

123.

124.

125.

126.

127.

128.

129.

130.

131.

132.

133.

134.

135.

136.

137.

138.

139.

140.

141.

142.

143.

144.

145.

146.

147.

148.

149.

150.

151.

152.

153.

154.

155.

156.

157.

158.

159.

160.

161.

162.

163.

164.

165.

166.

167.

168.

169.

170.

171.

172.

173.

174.

175.

176.

177.

178.

179.

180.

181. Major Projects - Goals Achieved: January

182. Major Projects - Goals Achieved: February

183. Major Projects - Goals Achieved: March

184. Major Projects - Goals Achieved: April

185. Major Projects - Goals Achieved: May

186. Major Projects - Goals Achieved: June

187. Major Projects - Goals Achieved: July

188. Major Projects - Goals Achieved: August

189. Major Projects - Goals Achieved: September

190. Major Projects - Goals Achieved: October

191. Major Projects - Goals Achieved: November

192. Major Projects - Goals Achieved: December

193. Continuing Education

194. Networking / Associations

195. Vendors

196. Contacts

197. Contacts

198. Contacts

199. Contacts

200. Contacts

Top 3 Work Tasks Today: Date:

❏

❏

❏

Information to Obtain / People to Contact:

❏

❏

❏

Documents to Obtain:

❏

❏

❏

Notes:

Top 3 Work Tasks Today: Date:

☐ _____

☐ _____

☐ _____

Information to Obtain / People to Contact:

☐ _____

☐ _____

☐ _____

Documents to Obtain:

☐ _____

☐ _____

☐ _____

Notes:

_____

_____

_____

_____

_____

_____

_____

_____

_____

Top 3 Work Tasks Today: Date:

❑ _____

❑ _____

❑ _____

Information to Obtain / People to Contact:

❑ _____

❑ _____

❑ _____

Documents to Obtain:

❑ _____

❑ _____

❑ _____

Notes:

_____

_____

_____

_____

_____

_____

_____

_____

_____

Top 3 Work Tasks Today: Date:

❑ _____

❑ _____

❑ _____

Information to Obtain / People to Contact:

❑ _____

❑ _____

❑ _____

Documents to Obtain:

❑ _____

❑ _____

❑ _____

Notes:

_____

_____

_____

_____

_____

_____

_____

_____

Top 3 Work Tasks Today: Date:

☐ _____

☐ _____

☐ _____

Information to Obtain / People to Contact:

☐ _____

☐ _____

☐ _____

Documents to Obtain:

☐ _____

☐ _____

☐ _____

Notes:

_____

_____

_____

_____

_____

_____

_____

_____

_____

_____

Top 3 Work Tasks Today:

Date:

❑

_____

❑

❑

Information to Obtain / People to Contact:

❑

❑

❑

Documents to Obtain:

❑

❑

❑

Notes:

Top 3 Work Tasks Today: Date:

❏

❏

❏

Information to Obtain / People to Contact:

❏

❏

❏

Documents to Obtain:

❏

❏

❏

Notes:

Top 3 Work Tasks Today: Date:

☐ _____

☐

☐

Information to Obtain / People to Contact:

☐

☐

☐

Documents to Obtain:

☐

☐

☐

Notes:

Top 3 Work Tasks Today: Date:

☐ _____   _____

☐ _____

☐ _____

Information to Obtain / People to Contact:

☐ _____

☐ _____

☐ _____

Documents to Obtain:

☐ _____

☐ _____

☐ _____

Notes:

_____

_____

_____

_____

_____

_____

_____

_____

_____

_____

Top 3 Work Tasks Today:

❏

Date:
_____

❏

❏

Information to Obtain / People to Contact:

❏

❏

❏

Documents to Obtain:

❏

❏

❏

Notes:

Top 3 Work Tasks Today: Date:

❑ _____

❑ _____

❑ _____

Information to Obtain / People to Contact:

❑ _____

❑ _____

❑ _____

Documents to Obtain:

❑ _____

❑ _____

❑ _____

Notes:

_____

_____

_____

_____

_____

_____

_____

_____

_____

Top 3 Work Tasks Today: Date:

❑

❑

❑

Information to Obtain / People to Contact:

❑

❑

❑

Documents to Obtain:

❑

❑

❑

Notes:

Top 3 Work Tasks Today: Date:

☐

☐

☐

Information to Obtain / People to Contact:

☐

☐

☐

Documents to Obtain:

☐

☐

☐

Notes:

Top 3 Work Tasks Today: Date:

☐ _____

☐ _____

☐ _____

Information to Obtain / People to Contact:

☐ _____

☐ _____

☐ _____

Documents to Obtain:

☐ _____

☐ _____

☐ _____

Notes:

_____

_____

_____

_____

_____

_____

_____

_____

Top 3 Work Tasks Today: Date:

❏ _____

❏

❏

Information to Obtain / People to Contact:

❏

❏

❏

Documents to Obtain:

❏

❏

❏

Notes:

Top 3 Work Tasks Today: Date:

❏ _____

❏ _____

❏ _____

Information to Obtain / People to Contact:

❏ _____

❏ _____

❏ _____

Documents to Obtain:

❏ _____

❏ _____

❏ _____

Notes:

_____

_____

_____

_____

_____

_____

_____

_____

_____

Top 3 Work Tasks Today: Date: _____

☐

☐

☐

Information to Obtain / People to Contact:

☐

☐

☐

Documents to Obtain:

☐

☐

☐

Notes:

_____

_____

_____

_____

_____

_____

_____

_____

_____

_____

_____

Top 3 Work Tasks Today: Date:

❑

_____

❑

_____

❑

_____

Information to Obtain / People to Contact:

❑

_____

❑

_____

❑

_____

Documents to Obtain:

❑

_____

❑

_____

❑

_____

Notes:

_____

_____

_____

_____

_____

_____

_____

_____

_____

Top 3 Work Tasks Today: Date:

❏ _____

❏ _____

❏ _____

Information to Obtain / People to Contact:

❏ _____

❏ _____

❏ _____

Documents to Obtain:

❏ _____

❏ _____

❏ _____

Notes:

_____

_____

_____

_____

_____

_____

_____

_____

_____

Top 3 Work Tasks Today: Date:

❏ _____

❏ _____

❏ _____

Information to Obtain / People to Contact:

❏ _____

❏ _____

❏ _____

Documents to Obtain:

❏ _____

❏ _____

❏ _____

Notes:

_____

_____

_____

_____

_____

_____

_____

_____

Top 3 Work Tasks Today: Date:

❑ _____

❑ _____

❑ _____

Information to Obtain / People to Contact:

❑ _____

❑ _____

❑ _____

Documents to Obtain:

❑ _____

❑ _____

❑ _____

Notes:

_____

_____

_____

_____

_____

_____

_____

_____

_____

Top 3 Work Tasks Today: Date:

❑ _____

❑ _____

❑ _____

Information to Obtain / People to Contact:

❑ _____

❑ _____

❑ _____

Documents to Obtain:

❑ _____

❑ _____

❑ _____

Notes:

_____

_____

_____

_____

_____

_____

_____

_____

Top 3 Work Tasks Today: Date:

☐ _____

☐ _____

☐ _____

Information to Obtain / People to Contact:

☐ _____

☐ _____

☐ _____

Documents to Obtain:

☐ _____

☐ _____

☐ _____

Notes:

_____

_____

_____

_____

_____

_____

_____

_____

_____

Top 3 Work Tasks Today:

❏

Date: _____

❏

❏

Information to Obtain / People to Contact:

❏

❏

❏

Documents to Obtain:

❏

❏

❏

Notes:

Top 3 Work Tasks Today: Date:

❏

❏

❏

Information to Obtain / People to Contact:

❏

❏

❏

Documents to Obtain:

❏

❏

❏

Notes:

Top 3 Work Tasks Today: Date:

❑ _____

❑

❑

Information to Obtain / People to Contact:

❑

❑

❑

Documents to Obtain:

❑

❑

❑

Notes:

Top 3 Work Tasks Today: Date:

❑ _____

❑ _____

❑ _____

Information to Obtain / People to Contact:

❑ _____

❑ _____

❑ _____

Documents to Obtain:

❑ _____

❑ _____

❑ _____

Notes:

_____

_____

_____

_____

_____

_____

_____

_____

Top 3 Work Tasks Today: Date:

❏

_____

❏

_____

❏

_____

Information to Obtain / People to Contact:

❏

_____

❏

_____

❏

_____

Documents to Obtain:

❏

_____

❏

_____

❏

_____

Notes:

_____

_____

_____

_____

_____

_____

_____

_____

_____

Top 3 Work Tasks Today: Date:

☐

_____

☐

_____

☐

_____

Information to Obtain / People to Contact:

☐

_____

☐

_____

☐

_____

Documents to Obtain:

☐

_____

☐

_____

☐

_____

Notes:

_____

_____

_____

_____

_____

_____

_____

_____

_____

_____

_____

Top 3 Work Tasks Today: Date:

❑ _____

❑ _____

❑ _____

Information to Obtain / People to Contact:

❑ _____

❑ _____

❑ _____

Documents to Obtain:

❑ _____

❑ _____

❑ _____

Notes:

_____

_____

_____

_____

_____

_____

_____

_____

Top 3 Work Tasks Today: Date:

❏ _____

❏ _____

❏ _____

Information to Obtain / People to Contact:

❏ _____

❏ _____

❏ _____

Documents to Obtain:

❏ _____

❏ _____

❏ _____

Notes:

_____

_____

_____

_____

_____

_____

_____

_____

_____

Top 3 Work Tasks Today: Date:

❑ _____

❑ _____

❑ _____

Information to Obtain / People to Contact:

❑ _____

❑ _____

❑ _____

Documents to Obtain:

❑ _____

❑ _____

❑ _____

Notes:

_____

_____

_____

_____

_____

_____

_____

_____

_____

Top 3 Work Tasks Today: Date:

☐

☐

☐

Information to Obtain / People to Contact:

☐

☐

☐

Documents to Obtain:

☐

☐

☐

Notes:

_____

_____

_____

_____

_____

_____

_____

_____

_____

_____

Top 3 Work Tasks Today: Date:

❑ _____

❑ _____

❑ _____

Information to Obtain / People to Contact:

❑ _____

❑ _____

❑ _____

Documents to Obtain:

❑ _____

❑ _____

❑ _____

Notes:

_____

_____

_____

_____

_____

_____

_____

_____

_____

Top 3 Work Tasks Today: Date:

☐

_____

☐

_____

☐

_____

Information to Obtain / People to Contact:

☐

_____

☐

_____

☐

_____

Documents to Obtain:

☐

_____

☐

_____

☐

_____

Notes:

_____

_____

_____

_____

_____

_____

_____

_____

_____

Top 3 Work Tasks Today: Date:

❑ _____

❑ _____

❑ _____

Information to Obtain / People to Contact:

❑ _____

❑ _____

❑ _____

Documents to Obtain:

❑ _____

❑ _____

❑ _____

Notes:

_____

_____

_____

_____

_____

_____

_____

_____

_____

Top 3 Work Tasks Today: Date:

❏ _____

❏ _____

❏ _____

Information to Obtain / People to Contact:

❏ _____

❏ _____

❏ _____

Documents to Obtain:

❏ _____

❏ _____

❏ _____

Notes:

_____

_____

_____

_____

_____

_____

_____

_____

_____

_____

Top 3 Work Tasks Today: Date:

❑ _____

❑ _____

❑ _____

Information to Obtain / People to Contact:

❑ _____

❑ _____

❑ _____

Documents to Obtain:

❑ _____

❑ _____

❑ _____

Notes:

_____

_____

_____

_____

_____

_____

_____

_____

_____

Top 3 Work Tasks Today: Date:

❏

❏

❏

Information to Obtain / People to Contact:

❏

❏

❏

Documents to Obtain:

❏

❏

❏

Notes:

Top 3 Work Tasks Today: Date:

❑ _____

❑ _____

❑ _____

Information to Obtain / People to Contact:

❑ _____

❑ _____

❑ _____

Documents to Obtain:

❑ _____

❑ _____

❑ _____

Notes:

_____

_____

_____

_____

_____

_____

_____

_____

_____

Top 3 Work Tasks Today: Date:

❏ _____

❏ _____

❏ _____

Information to Obtain / People to Contact:

❏ _____

❏ _____

❏ _____

Documents to Obtain:

❏ _____

❏ _____

❏ _____

Notes:

_____

_____

_____

_____

_____

_____

_____

_____

_____

_____

Top 3 Work Tasks Today: Date:

❑

❑

❑

Information to Obtain / People to Contact:

❑

❑

❑

Documents to Obtain:

❑

❑

❑

Notes:

Top 3 Work Tasks Today: Date:

❏

❏

❏

Information to Obtain / People to Contact:

❏

❏

❏

Documents to Obtain:

❏

❏

❏

Notes:

Top 3 Work Tasks Today: Date:

☐ _____

☐ _____

☐ _____

Information to Obtain / People to Contact:

☐ _____

☐ _____

☐ _____

Documents to Obtain:

☐ _____

☐ _____

☐ _____

Notes:

_____

_____

_____

_____

_____

_____

_____

_____

Top 3 Work Tasks Today:　　　　　　　　　　　　　Date: _____

❏

❏

❏

Information to Obtain / People to Contact:

❏

❏

❏

Documents to Obtain:

❏

❏

❏

Notes:

Top 3 Work Tasks Today: Date:

☐ _____

☐ _____

☐ _____

Information to Obtain / People to Contact:

☐ _____

☐ _____

☐ _____

Documents to Obtain:

☐ _____

☐ _____

☐ _____

Notes:

_____

_____

_____

_____

_____

_____

_____

_____

Top 3 Work Tasks Today:

Date:

❏ _____

❏ _____

❏ _____

Information to Obtain / People to Contact:

❏ _____

❏ _____

❏ _____

Documents to Obtain:

❏ _____

❏ _____

❏ _____

Notes:

_____

_____

_____

_____

_____

_____

_____

_____

_____

_____

Top 3 Work Tasks Today: Date:

❑ _____

❑ _____

❑ _____

Information to Obtain / People to Contact:

❑ _____

❑ _____

❑ _____

Documents to Obtain:

❑ _____

❑ _____

❑ _____

Notes:

_____

_____

_____

_____

_____

_____

_____

_____

Top 3 Work Tasks Today: Date:

❑

❑

❑

Information to Obtain / People to Contact:

❑

❑

❑

Documents to Obtain:

❑

❑

❑

Notes:

Top 3 Work Tasks Today: Date:

❏

_____

❏

❏

Information to Obtain / People to Contact:

❏

❏

❏

Documents to Obtain:

❏

❏

❏

Notes:

Top 3 Work Tasks Today: Date:

☐

☐ _____

☐ _____

_____

Information to Obtain / People to Contact:

☐

☐ _____

☐ _____

_____

Documents to Obtain:

☐

☐ _____

☐ _____

_____

Notes:

_____

_____

_____

_____

_____

_____

_____

_____

_____

_____

Top 3 Work Tasks Today: Date:

☐ _____

☐ _____

☐ _____

Information to Obtain / People to Contact:

☐ _____

☐ _____

☐ _____

Documents to Obtain:

☐ _____

☐ _____

☐ _____

Notes:

_____

_____

_____

_____

_____

_____

_____

_____

Top 3 Work Tasks Today:

☐

Date:
_____

☐

☐

Information to Obtain / People to Contact:

☐

☐

☐

Documents to Obtain:

☐

☐

☐

Notes:

Top 3 Work Tasks Today: Date:

❑ _____

❑

❑

Information to Obtain / People to Contact:

❑

❑

❑

Documents to Obtain:

❑

❑

❑

Notes:

Top 3 Work Tasks Today: Date:

- ❏
- ❏
- ❏

Information to Obtain / People to Contact:

- ❏
- ❏
- ❏

Documents to Obtain:

- ❏
- ❏
- ❏

Notes:

Top 3 Work Tasks Today: Date:

❑ _____

❑ _____

❑ _____

Information to Obtain / People to Contact:

❑ _____

❑ _____

❑ _____

Documents to Obtain:

❑ _____

❑ _____

❑ _____

Notes:

_____

_____

_____

_____

_____

_____

_____

_____

Top 3 Work Tasks Today: Date:

☐ _____

☐ _____

☐ _____

Information to Obtain / People to Contact:

☐ _____

☐ _____

☐ _____

Documents to Obtain:

☐ _____

☐ _____

☐ _____

Notes:

_____

_____

_____

_____

_____

_____

_____

_____

_____

Top 3 Work Tasks Today:

☐

Date:
_____

☐

☐

Information to Obtain / People to Contact:

☐

☐

☐

Documents to Obtain:

☐

☐

☐

Notes:

Top 3 Work Tasks Today: Date:

☐

_____

☐

_____

☐

_____

Information to Obtain / People to Contact:

☐

_____

☐

_____

☐

_____

Documents to Obtain:

☐

_____

☐

_____

☐

_____

Notes:

_____

_____

_____

_____

_____

_____

_____

_____

_____

_____

Top 3 Work Tasks Today: Date:

❑

_____

❑

_____

❑

_____

Information to Obtain / People to Contact:

❑

_____

❑

_____

❑

_____

Documents to Obtain:

❑

_____

❑

_____

❑

_____

Notes:

_____

_____

_____

_____

_____

_____

_____

_____

_____

_____

Top 3 Work Tasks Today: Date:

❏ _____

❏ _____

❏ _____

Information to Obtain / People to Contact:

❏ _____

❏ _____

❏ _____

Documents to Obtain:

❏ _____

❏ _____

❏ _____

Notes:

_____

_____

_____

_____

_____

_____

_____

_____

_____

_____

Top 3 Work Tasks Today: Date:

❑ _____

❑ _____

❑ _____

Information to Obtain / People to Contact:

❑ _____

❑ _____

❑ _____

Documents to Obtain:

❑ _____

❑ _____

❑ _____

Notes:

_____

_____

_____

_____

_____

_____

_____

_____

Top 3 Work Tasks Today:

❑

Date:
_____

❑
_____

❑
_____

Information to Obtain / People to Contact:

❑
_____

❑
_____

❑
_____

Documents to Obtain:

❑
_____

❑
_____

❑
_____

Notes:

_____

_____

_____

_____

_____

_____

_____

_____

Top 3 Work Tasks Today: Date:

❑ _____

❑ _____

❑ _____

Information to Obtain / People to Contact:

❑ _____

❑ _____

❑ _____

Documents to Obtain:

❑ _____

❑ _____

❑ _____

Notes:

_____

_____

_____

_____

_____

_____

_____

_____

Top 3 Work Tasks Today:

Date: _____

☐

☐

☐

Information to Obtain / People to Contact:

☐

☐

☐

Documents to Obtain:

☐

☐

☐

Notes:

Top 3 Work Tasks Today: Date:

❑ _____

❑ _____

❑ _____

Information to Obtain / People to Contact:

❑ _____

❑ _____

❑ _____

Documents to Obtain:

❑ _____

❑ _____

❑ _____

Notes:

_____

_____

_____

_____

_____

_____

_____

_____

Top 3 Work Tasks Today: Date:

☐ _____

☐ _____

☐ _____

Information to Obtain / People to Contact:

☐ _____

☐ _____

☐ _____

Documents to Obtain:

☐ _____

☐ _____

☐ _____

Notes:

_____

_____

_____

_____

_____

_____

_____

_____

_____

_____

Top 3 Work Tasks Today: Date:

❑ _____

❑ _____

❑ _____

Information to Obtain / People to Contact:

❑ _____

❑ _____

❑ _____

Documents to Obtain:

❑ _____

❑ _____

❑ _____

Notes:

_____

_____

_____

_____

_____

_____

_____

Top 3 Work Tasks Today: Date:

❑ _____

❑ _____

❑ _____

Information to Obtain / People to Contact:

❑ _____

❑ _____

❑ _____

Documents to Obtain:

❑ _____

❑ _____

❑ _____

Notes:

_____

_____

_____

_____

_____

_____

_____

_____

_____

Top 3 Work Tasks Today: Date:

❏ _____

❏ _____

❏ _____

Information to Obtain / People to Contact:

❏ _____

❏ _____

❏ _____

Documents to Obtain:

❏ _____

❏ _____

❏ _____

Notes:

_____

_____

_____

_____

_____

_____

_____

_____

_____

Top 3 Work Tasks Today: Date:

❑ _____

❑ _____

❑ _____

Information to Obtain / People to Contact:

❑ _____

❑ _____

❑ _____

Documents to Obtain:

❑ _____

❑ _____

❑ _____

Notes:

_____

_____

_____

_____

_____

_____

_____

_____

_____

_____

Top 3 Work Tasks Today: Date:

❑ _____

❑ _____

❑ _____

Information to Obtain / People to Contact:

❑ _____

❑ _____

❑ _____

Documents to Obtain:

❑ _____

❑ _____

❑ _____

Notes:

_____

_____

_____

_____

_____

_____

_____

_____

_____

Top 3 Work Tasks Today:

Date: _____

❏

❏

❏

Information to Obtain / People to Contact:

❏

❏

❏

Documents to Obtain:

❏

❏

❏

Notes:

Top 3 Work Tasks Today: Date:

❑ _____

❑

❑

Information to Obtain / People to Contact:

❑

❑

❑

Documents to Obtain:

❑

❑

❑

Notes:

Top 3 Work Tasks Today: Date:

❑

❑

❑

Information to Obtain / People to Contact:

❑

❑

❑

Documents to Obtain:

❑

❑

❑

Notes:

Top 3 Work Tasks Today: Date:

❑ _____

❑ _____

❑ _____

Information to Obtain / People to Contact:

❑ _____

❑ _____

❑ _____

Documents to Obtain:

❑ _____

❑ _____

❑ _____

Notes:

_____

_____

_____

_____

_____

_____

_____

_____

Top 3 Work Tasks Today: Date:

☐

☐

☐

Information to Obtain / People to Contact:

☐

☐

☐

Documents to Obtain:

☐

☐

☐

Notes:

Top 3 Work Tasks Today: Date:

❑ _____

❑ _____

❑ _____

Information to Obtain / People to Contact:

❑ _____

❑ _____

❑ _____

Documents to Obtain:

❑ _____

❑ _____

❑ _____

Notes:

_____

_____

_____

_____

_____

_____

_____

_____

Top 3 Work Tasks Today: Date:

❏

❏
_____

❏
_____

Information to Obtain / People to Contact:

❏
_____

❏
_____

❏
_____

Documents to Obtain:

❏
_____

❏
_____

❏
_____

Notes:
_____
_____
_____
_____
_____
_____
_____
_____
_____

Top 3 Work Tasks Today: Date:

❏

❏

❏

Information to Obtain / People to Contact:

❏

❏

❏

Documents to Obtain:

❏

❏

❏

Notes:

Top 3 Work Tasks Today: Date:

☐ _____

☐ _____

☐ _____

Information to Obtain / People to Contact:

☐ _____

☐ _____

☐ _____

Documents to Obtain:

☐ _____

☐ _____

☐ _____

Notes:

_____

_____

_____

_____

_____

_____

_____

_____

_____

Top 3 Work Tasks Today: Date:

❏ _____

❏ _____

❏ _____

Information to Obtain / People to Contact:

❏ _____

❏ _____

❏ _____

Documents to Obtain:

❏ _____

❏ _____

❏ _____

Notes:

_____

_____

_____

_____

_____

_____

_____

_____

Top 3 Work Tasks Today: Date:

☐ _____

☐ _____

☐ _____

Information to Obtain / People to Contact:

☐ _____

☐ _____

☐ _____

Documents to Obtain:

☐ _____

☐ _____

☐ _____

Notes:

_____

_____

_____

_____

_____

_____

_____

_____

_____

_____

_____

Top 3 Work Tasks Today: Date:

❑ _____

❑ _____

❑ _____

Information to Obtain / People to Contact:

❑ _____

❑ _____

❑ _____

Documents to Obtain:

❑ _____

❑ _____

❑ _____

Notes:

_____

_____

_____

_____

_____

_____

_____

_____

Top 3 Work Tasks Today: Date:

❏

❏

❏

Information to Obtain / People to Contact:

❏

❏

❏

Documents to Obtain:

❏

❏

❏

Notes:

Top 3 Work Tasks Today: Date:

❑ _____

❑

❑

Information to Obtain / People to Contact:

❑

❑

❑

Documents to Obtain:

❑

❑

❑

Notes:

❑ Top 3 Work Tasks Today: Date:
                                        _____

❑ _____

❑ _____

❑ Information to Obtain / People to Contact:

❑ _____

❑ _____

❑ Documents to Obtain:

❑ _____

❑ _____

Notes:

_____

_____

_____

_____

_____

_____

_____

_____

_____

_____

Top 3 Work Tasks Today: Date:

☐ _____

☐ _____

☐ _____

Information to Obtain / People to Contact:

☐ _____

☐ _____

☐ _____

Documents to Obtain:

☐ _____

☐ _____

☐ _____

Notes:

_____

_____

_____

_____

_____

_____

_____

_____

_____

Top 3 Work Tasks Today: Date:

☐ _____

☐ _____

☐ _____

Information to Obtain / People to Contact:

☐ _____

☐ _____

☐ _____

Documents to Obtain:

☐ _____

☐ _____

☐ _____

Notes:

_____

_____

_____

_____

_____

_____

_____

_____

_____

_____

Top 3 Work Tasks Today: Date:

❑

_____

❑

_____

❑

_____

Information to Obtain / People to Contact:

❑

_____

❑

_____

Documents to Obtain:

❑

_____

❑

_____

Notes:

_____

_____

_____

_____

_____

_____

_____

_____

_____

Top 3 Work Tasks Today: Date:

❏ _____

❏ _____

❏ _____

Information to Obtain / People to Contact:

❏ _____

❏ _____

❏ _____

Documents to Obtain:

❏ _____

❏ _____

❏ _____

Notes:

_____

_____

_____

_____

_____

_____

_____

_____

_____

_____

Top 3 Work Tasks Today: Date:

❑

_____

❑

_____

❑

_____

Information to Obtain / People to Contact:

❑

_____

❑

_____

❑

_____

Documents to Obtain:

❑

_____

❑

_____

❑

_____

Notes:

_____

_____

_____

_____

_____

_____

_____

_____

_____

Top 3 Work Tasks Today: Date:

❑ _____

❑ _____

❑ _____

Information to Obtain / People to Contact:

❑ _____

❑ _____

❑ _____

Documents to Obtain:

❑ _____

❑ _____

❑ _____

Notes:

_____

_____

_____

_____

_____

_____

_____

_____

Top 3 Work Tasks Today: Date:

☐ _____

☐ _____

☐ _____

Information to Obtain / People to Contact:

☐ _____

☐ _____

☐ _____

Documents to Obtain:

☐ _____

☐ _____

☐ _____

Notes:

_____

_____

_____

_____

_____

_____

_____

_____

Top 3 Work Tasks Today: Date:
☐ _____

☐ _____

☐ _____

Information to Obtain / People to Contact:
☐

☐ _____

☐ _____

Documents to Obtain:
☐

☐ _____

☐ _____

Notes:
_____
_____
_____
_____
_____
_____
_____
_____
_____
_____

Top 3 Work Tasks Today: Date:

❑

❑

❑

Information to Obtain / People to Contact:

❑

❑

❑

Documents to Obtain:

❑

❑

❑

Notes:

Top 3 Work Tasks Today: Date:

❏ _____

❏ _____

❏ _____

Information to Obtain / People to Contact:

❏ _____

❏ _____

❏ _____

Documents to Obtain:

❏ _____

❏ _____

❏ _____

Notes:

_____

_____

_____

_____

_____

_____

_____

_____

_____

_____

Top 3 Work Tasks Today: Date:

☐ _____

☐ _____

☐ _____

Information to Obtain / People to Contact:

☐ _____

☐ _____

☐ _____

Documents to Obtain:

☐ _____

☐ _____

☐ _____

Notes:

_____

_____

_____

_____

_____

_____

_____

_____

Top 3 Work Tasks Today: Date:

❑ _____

❑ _____

❑ _____

Information to Obtain / People to Contact:

❑ _____

❑ _____

❑ _____

Documents to Obtain:

❑ _____

❑ _____

❑ _____

Notes:

_____

_____

_____

_____

_____

_____

_____

_____

_____

Top 3 Work Tasks Today: Date:

❑

❑

❑

Information to Obtain / People to Contact:

❑

❑

❑

Documents to Obtain:

❑

❑

❑

Notes:

Top 3 Work Tasks Today:

☐

Date:
_____

☐
_____

☐
_____

_____

Information to Obtain / People to Contact:

☐
_____

☐
_____

☐
_____

_____

Documents to Obtain:

☐
_____

☐
_____

☐
_____

_____

Notes:

_____

_____

_____

_____

_____

_____

_____

_____

_____

_____

Top 3 Work Tasks Today: Date:

❑

_____

❑

_____

❑

_____

Information to Obtain / People to Contact:

❑

_____

❑

_____

❑

_____

Documents to Obtain:

❑

_____

❑

_____

❑

_____

Notes:

_____

_____

_____

_____

_____

_____

_____

_____

_____

_____

Top 3 Work Tasks Today: Date:

❏

❏

❏

Information to Obtain / People to Contact:

❏

❏

❏

Documents to Obtain:

❏

❏

❏

Notes:

Top 3 Work Tasks Today: Date:

❑ _____

❑ _____

❑ _____

Information to Obtain / People to Contact:

❑ _____

❑ _____

❑ _____

Documents to Obtain:

❑ _____

❑ _____

❑ _____

Notes:

_____

_____

_____

_____

_____

_____

_____

_____

_____

Top 3 Work Tasks Today:

☐

Date: _____

☐

☐

Information to Obtain / People to Contact:

☐

☐

☐

Documents to Obtain:

☐

☐

☐

Notes:

Top 3 Work Tasks Today: Date:

❑ _____

❑ _____

❑ _____

Information to Obtain / People to Contact:

❑ _____

❑ _____

❑ _____

Documents to Obtain:

❑ _____

❑ _____

❑ _____

Notes:

_____

_____

_____

_____

_____

_____

_____

_____

_____

Top 3 Work Tasks Today: Date:

☐ _____

☐ _____

☐ _____

Information to Obtain / People to Contact:

☐ _____

☐ _____

☐ _____

Documents to Obtain:

☐ _____

☐ _____

☐ _____

Notes:

_____

_____

_____

_____

_____

_____

_____

_____

_____

_____

Top 3 Work Tasks Today: Date:

❑ _____

❑ _____

❑ _____

Information to Obtain / People to Contact:

❑ _____

❑ _____

❑ _____

Documents to Obtain:

❑ _____

❑ _____

❑ _____

Notes:

_____

_____

_____

_____

_____

_____

_____

_____

_____

Top 3 Work Tasks Today: Date:

❏

_____

❏

_____

❏

_____

Information to Obtain / People to Contact:

❏

_____

❏

_____

❏

_____

Documents to Obtain:

❏

_____

❏

_____

❏

_____

Notes:

_____

_____

_____

_____

_____

_____

_____

_____

_____

_____

Top 3 Work Tasks Today: Date:

❑ _____

❑ _____

❑ _____

Information to Obtain / People to Contact:

❑ _____

❑ _____

❑ _____

Documents to Obtain:

❑ _____

❑ _____

❑ _____

Notes:

_____

_____

_____

_____

_____

_____

_____

_____

_____

Top 3 Work Tasks Today: Date:

❏

❏

❏

Information to Obtain / People to Contact:

❏

❏

❏

Documents to Obtain:

❏

❏

❏

Notes:

Top 3 Work Tasks Today:

❏

❏

❏

Information to Obtain / People to Contact:

❏

❏

❏

Documents to Obtain:

❏

❏

❏

Notes:

Top 3 Work Tasks Today: Date:
☐ _____

☐ _____

☐ _____

Information to Obtain / People to Contact:
☐ _____

☐ _____

☐ _____

Documents to Obtain:
☐ _____

☐ _____

☐ _____

Notes:
_____

_____

_____

_____

_____

_____

_____

_____

_____

_____

Top 3 Work Tasks Today: Date:

❑ _____

❑ _____

❑ _____

Information to Obtain / People to Contact:

❑ _____

❑ _____

❑ _____

Documents to Obtain:

❑ _____

❑ _____

❑ _____

Notes:

_____

_____

_____

_____

_____

_____

_____

_____

Top 3 Work Tasks Today: Date:

❏

❏ _____

❏ _____

Information to Obtain / People to Contact:

❏

❏ _____

❏ _____

Documents to Obtain:

❏

❏ _____

❏ _____

Notes:

_____

_____

_____

_____

_____

_____

_____

_____

_____

_____

_____

Top 3 Work Tasks Today: Date:

❑ _____

❑

❑

Information to Obtain / People to Contact:

❑

❑

❑

Documents to Obtain:

❑

❑

❑

Notes:

Top 3 Work Tasks Today: Date:

❑ _____

❑ _____

❑ _____

Information to Obtain / People to Contact:

❑ _____

❑ _____

❑ _____

Documents to Obtain:

❑ _____

❑ _____

❑ _____

Notes:

_____

_____

_____

_____

_____

_____

_____

_____

_____

_____

Top 3 Work Tasks Today: Date:

❑ _____

❑ _____

❑ _____

Information to Obtain / People to Contact:

❑ _____

❑ _____

❑ _____

Documents to Obtain:

❑ _____

❑ _____

❑ _____

Notes:

_____

_____

_____

_____

_____

_____

_____

_____

Top 3 Work Tasks Today: Date:
☐ _____

☐ _____

☐ _____

Information to Obtain / People to Contact:
☐ _____

☐ _____

☐ _____

Documents to Obtain:
☐ _____

☐ _____

☐ _____

Notes:
_____
_____
_____
_____
_____
_____
_____
_____
_____

Top 3 Work Tasks Today: Date:

☐ _____

☐ _____

☐ _____

Information to Obtain / People to Contact:

☐ _____

☐ _____

☐ _____

Documents to Obtain:

☐ _____

☐ _____

☐ _____

Notes:

_____

_____

_____

_____

_____

_____

_____

_____

Top 3 Work Tasks Today: Date:

❏ _____

❏ _____

❏ _____

Information to Obtain / People to Contact:

❏ _____

❏ _____

❏ _____

Documents to Obtain:

❏ _____

❏ _____

❏ _____

Notes:

_____

_____

_____

_____

_____

_____

_____

_____

_____

_____

Top 3 Work Tasks Today: Date:

❑ _____

❑ _____

❑ _____

Information to Obtain / People to Contact:

❑ _____

❑ _____

❑ _____

Documents to Obtain:

❑ _____

❑ _____

❑ _____

Notes:

_____

_____

_____

_____

_____

_____

_____

_____

Top 3 Work Tasks Today: Date:

❏ _____

❏ _____

❏ _____

Information to Obtain / People to Contact:

❏ _____

❏ _____

❏ _____

Documents to Obtain:

❏ _____

❏ _____

❏ _____

Notes:

_____

_____

_____

_____

_____

_____

_____

_____

_____

Top 3 Work Tasks Today: Date:

❏

❏

❏

Information to Obtain / People to Contact:

❏

❏

❏

Documents to Obtain:

❏

❏

❏

Notes:

Top 3 Work Tasks Today:

Date: _____

☐

☐

☐

Information to Obtain / People to Contact:

☐

☐

☐

Documents to Obtain:

☐

☐

☐

Notes:

Top 3 Work Tasks Today: Date:
❑ _____

❑ _____

❑ _____

Information to Obtain / People to Contact:
❑ _____

❑ _____

❑ _____

Documents to Obtain:
❑ _____

❑ _____

❑ _____

Notes:
_____

_____

_____

_____

_____

_____

_____

_____

Top 3 Work Tasks Today: Date:

❏ _____

❏ _____

❏ _____

Information to Obtain / People to Contact:

❏ _____

❏ _____

❏ _____

Documents to Obtain:

❏ _____

❏ _____

❏ _____

Notes:

_____

_____

_____

_____

_____

_____

_____

_____

_____

_____

Top 3 Work Tasks Today: Date:

❏ _____

❏ _____

❏ _____

Information to Obtain / People to Contact:

❏ _____

❏ _____

❏ _____

Documents to Obtain:

❏ _____

❏ _____

❏ _____

Notes:

_____

_____

_____

_____

_____

_____

_____

_____

Top 3 Work Tasks Today: Date:

☐

☐ _____

☐ _____

Information to Obtain / People to Contact:

☐

☐ _____

☐ _____

Documents to Obtain:

☐

☐ _____

☐ _____

Notes:

_____

_____

_____

_____

_____

_____

_____

_____

Top 3 Work Tasks Today: Date:

❑ _____

❑ _____

❑ _____

Information to Obtain / People to Contact:

❑ _____

❑ _____

❑ _____

Documents to Obtain:

❑ _____

❑ _____

❑ _____

Notes:

_____

_____

_____

_____

_____

_____

_____

_____

_____

Top 3 Work Tasks Today:

Date:
_____

❑

❑

❑

Information to Obtain / People to Contact:

❑

❑

❑

Documents to Obtain:

❑

❑

❑

Notes:

Top 3 Work Tasks Today: Date:

❑ _____

❑ _____

❑ _____

Information to Obtain / People to Contact:

❑ _____

❑ _____

❑ _____

Documents to Obtain:

❑ _____

❑ _____

❑ _____

Notes:

_____

_____

_____

_____

_____

_____

_____

_____

Top 3 Work Tasks Today: Date:

❏ _____

❏ _____

❏ _____

Information to Obtain / People to Contact:

❏ _____

❏ _____

❏ _____

Documents to Obtain:

❏ _____

❏ _____

❏ _____

Notes:

_____

_____

_____

_____

_____

_____

_____

_____

_____

_____

Top 3 Work Tasks Today:

Date:

❑

❑

❑

Information to Obtain / People to Contact:

❑

❑

❑

Documents to Obtain:

❑

❑

❑

Notes:

Top 3 Work Tasks Today: Date:

☐

_____

☐

_____

☐

_____

Information to Obtain / People to Contact:

☐

_____

☐

_____

☐

_____

Documents to Obtain:

☐

_____

☐

_____

☐

_____

Notes:

_____

_____

_____

_____

_____

_____

_____

_____

_____

Top 3 Work Tasks Today: Date:

☐ _____

☐ _____

☐ _____

Information to Obtain / People to Contact:

☐ _____

☐ _____

☐ _____

Documents to Obtain:

☐ _____

☐ _____

☐ _____

Notes:

_____

_____

_____

_____

_____

_____

_____

_____

Top 3 Work Tasks Today:

❑

Date: _____

❑

❑

Information to Obtain / People to Contact:

❑

❑

❑

Documents to Obtain:

❑

❑

❑

Notes:

Top 3 Work Tasks Today: Date:

❑ _____

❑ _____

❑ _____

Information to Obtain / People to Contact:

❑ _____

❑ _____

❑ _____

Documents to Obtain:

❑ _____

❑ _____

❑ _____

Notes:

_____

_____

_____

_____

_____

_____

_____

_____

_____

Top 3 Work Tasks Today: Date:

❏

❏

❏

Information to Obtain / People to Contact:

❏

❏

❏

Documents to Obtain:

❏

❏

❏

Notes:

Top 3 Work Tasks Today: Date:

❑

❑

❑

Information to Obtain / People to Contact:

❑

❑

❑

Documents to Obtain:

❑

❑

❑

Notes:

☐ Top 3 Work Tasks Today: Date:
_____

☐ _____

☐ _____

☐ Information to Obtain / People to Contact:

☐ _____

☐ _____

☐ Documents to Obtain:

☐ _____

☐ _____

Notes:

_____

_____

_____

_____

_____

_____

_____

_____

_____

_____

Top 3 Work Tasks Today: Date:

❑ _____

❑ _____

❑ _____

Information to Obtain / People to Contact:

❑ _____

❑ _____

❑ _____

Documents to Obtain:

❑ _____

❑ _____

❑ _____

Notes:

_____

_____

_____

_____

_____

_____

_____

_____

Top 3 Work Tasks Today: Date:

❏ _____

❏ _____

❏ _____

Information to Obtain / People to Contact:

❏ _____

❏ _____

❏ _____

Documents to Obtain:

❏ _____

❏ _____

❏ _____

Notes:

_____

_____

_____

_____

_____

_____

_____

_____

_____

Top 3 Work Tasks Today: Date:

❑ _____

❑ _____

❑ _____

Information to Obtain / People to Contact:

❑ _____

❑ _____

❑ _____

Documents to Obtain:

❑ _____

❑ _____

❑ _____

Notes:

_____

_____

_____

_____

_____

_____

_____

_____

Top 3 Work Tasks Today: Date:

❏

_____

❏
_____

❏
_____
_____

Information to Obtain / People to Contact:

❏
_____

❏
_____

❏
_____
_____

Documents to Obtain:

❏
_____

❏
_____

❏
_____
_____

Notes:
_____
_____
_____
_____
_____
_____
_____
_____
_____
_____

Top 3 Work Tasks Today: Date:

☐ _____

☐ _____

☐ _____

Information to Obtain / People to Contact:

☐ _____

☐ _____

☐ _____

Documents to Obtain:

☐ _____

☐ _____

☐ _____

Notes:

_____

_____

_____

_____

_____

_____

_____

_____

_____

Top 3 Work Tasks Today: Date:

❑ _____

❑ _____

❑ _____

Information to Obtain / People to Contact:

❑ _____

❑ _____

❑ _____

Documents to Obtain:

❑ _____

❑ _____

❑ _____

Notes:

_____

_____

_____

_____

_____

_____

_____

_____

Top 3 Work Tasks Today: Date:

❑

❑

❑

Information to Obtain / People to Contact:

❑

❑

❑

Documents to Obtain:

❑

❑

❑

Notes:

Top 3 Work Tasks Today: Date:

☐

☐

☐

Information to Obtain / People to Contact:

☐

☐

☐

Documents to Obtain:

☐

☐

☐

Notes:

Top 3 Work Tasks Today: Date:

❏ _____ _____

❏ _____

❏ _____

Information to Obtain / People to Contact:

❏ _____

❏ _____

❏ _____

Documents to Obtain:

❏ _____

❏ _____

❏ _____

Notes:

_____

_____

_____

_____

_____

_____

_____

_____

_____

Top 3 Work Tasks Today: Date:

☐ _____

☐ _____

☐ _____

Information to Obtain / People to Contact:

☐ _____

☐ _____

☐ _____

Documents to Obtain:

☐ _____

☐ _____

☐ _____

Notes:

_____

_____

_____

_____

_____

_____

_____

_____

_____

_____

Top 3 Work Tasks Today: Date:

❑

❑

❑

Information to Obtain / People to Contact:

❑

❑

❑

Documents to Obtain:

❑

❑

❑

Notes:

Top 3 Work Tasks Today: Date:

❑

❑ _____

❑ _____

Information to Obtain / People to Contact:

❑

❑ _____

❑ _____

Documents to Obtain:

❑

❑ _____

❑ _____

Notes:

_____

_____

_____

_____

_____

_____

_____

_____

Top 3 Work Tasks Today: Date:

☐ _____

☐ _____

☐ _____

Information to Obtain / People to Contact:

☐ _____

☐ _____

☐ _____

Documents to Obtain:

☐ _____

☐ _____

☐ _____

Notes:

_____

_____

_____

_____

_____

_____

_____

_____

Top 3 Work Tasks Today: Date:

❏ _____

❏ _____

❏ _____

Information to Obtain / People to Contact:

❏ _____

❏ _____

❏ _____

Documents to Obtain:

❏ _____

❏ _____

❏ _____

Notes:

_____

_____

_____

_____

_____

_____

_____

_____

_____

_____

Top 3 Work Tasks Today: Date:

❑ _____

❑ _____

❑ _____

Information to Obtain / People to Contact:

❑ _____

❑ _____

❑ _____

Documents to Obtain:

❑ _____

❑ _____

❑ _____

Notes:

_____

_____

_____

_____

_____

_____

_____

_____

_____

Top 3 Work Tasks Today: Date:

❏ _____

❏ _____

❏ _____

Information to Obtain / People to Contact:

❏ _____

❏ _____

❏ _____

Documents to Obtain:

❏ _____

❏ _____

❏ _____

Notes:

_____

_____

_____

_____

_____

_____

_____

_____

_____

_____

Top 3 Work Tasks Today: Date:

☐

☐
_____

☐
_____

Information to Obtain / People to Contact:

☐

☐
_____

☐
_____

Documents to Obtain:

☐

☐
_____

☐
_____

Notes:

_____

_____

_____

_____

_____

_____

_____

_____

_____

Top 3 Work Tasks Today: Date:

☐

_____

☐

_____

☐

_____

Information to Obtain / People to Contact:

☐

_____

☐

_____

☐

_____

Documents to Obtain:

☐

_____

☐

_____

☐

_____

Notes:

_____

_____

_____

_____

_____

_____

_____

_____

_____

_____

Top 3 Work Tasks Today: Date:

❏ _____

❏ _____

❏ _____

Information to Obtain / People to Contact:

❏ _____

❏ _____

❏ _____

Documents to Obtain:

❏ _____

❏ _____

❏ _____

Notes:

_____

_____

_____

_____

_____

_____

_____

_____

Top 3 Work Tasks Today:

Date:

☐

☐

☐

Information to Obtain / People to Contact:

☐

☐

☐

Documents to Obtain:

☐

☐

☐

Notes:

Top 3 Work Tasks Today: Date:

❏ _____

❏ _____

❏ _____

Information to Obtain / People to Contact:

❏ _____

❏ _____

❏ _____

Documents to Obtain:

❏ _____

❏ _____

❏ _____

Notes:

_____

_____

_____

_____

_____

_____

_____

_____

_____

Top 3 Work Tasks Today: Date:

❏ _____

❏ _____

❏ _____

Information to Obtain / People to Contact:

❏ _____

❏ _____

❏ _____

Documents to Obtain:

❏ _____

❏ _____

❏ _____

Notes:

_____

_____

_____

_____

_____

_____

_____

_____

_____

Top 3 Work Tasks Today: Date:

☐ _____

☐ _____

☐ _____

Information to Obtain / People to Contact:

☐ _____

☐ _____

☐ _____

Documents to Obtain:

☐ _____

☐ _____

☐ _____

Notes:

_____

_____

_____

_____

_____

_____

_____

_____

Top 3 Work Tasks Today: Date:

☐ _____

☐ _____

☐ _____

Information to Obtain / People to Contact:

☐ _____

☐ _____

☐ _____

Documents to Obtain:

☐ _____

☐ _____

☐ _____

Notes:

_____

_____

_____

_____

_____

_____

_____

_____

_____

Top 3 Work Tasks Today: Date:

☐ _____

☐ _____

☐ _____

Information to Obtain / People to Contact:

☐ _____

☐ _____

☐ _____

Documents to Obtain:

☐ _____

☐ _____

☐ _____

Notes:

_____

_____

_____

_____

_____

_____

_____

_____

Top 3 Work Tasks Today: Date:

❏ _____

❏ _____

❏ _____

Information to Obtain / People to Contact:

❏ _____

❏ _____

❏ _____

Documents to Obtain:

❏ _____

❏ _____

❏ _____

Notes:

_____

_____

_____

_____

_____

_____

_____

_____

_____

Top 3 Work Tasks Today: Date:

❑ _____

❑ _____

❑ _____

Information to Obtain / People to Contact:

❑ _____

❑ _____

❑ _____

Documents to Obtain:

❑ _____

❑ _____

❑ _____

Notes:

_____

_____

_____

_____

_____

_____

_____

_____

Major Projects - Goals Achieved: January

Major Projects - Goals Achieved: February

Major Projects - Goals Achieved: March

Major Projects - Goals Achieved: April

Major Projects - Goals Achieved: May

Major Projects - Goals Achieved: June

Major Projects - Goals Achieved: July

Major Projects - Goals Achieved: August

Major Projects - Goals Achieved: September

Major Projects - Goals Achieved: October

Major Projects - Goals Achieved: November

Major Projects - Goals Achieved: December

Continuing Education

Networking / Associations

Vendors

Contacts

Contacts

Contacts

Contents

Contents

Contacts

Made in the USA
Las Vegas, NV
21 December 2020